Splinters

&

Streams

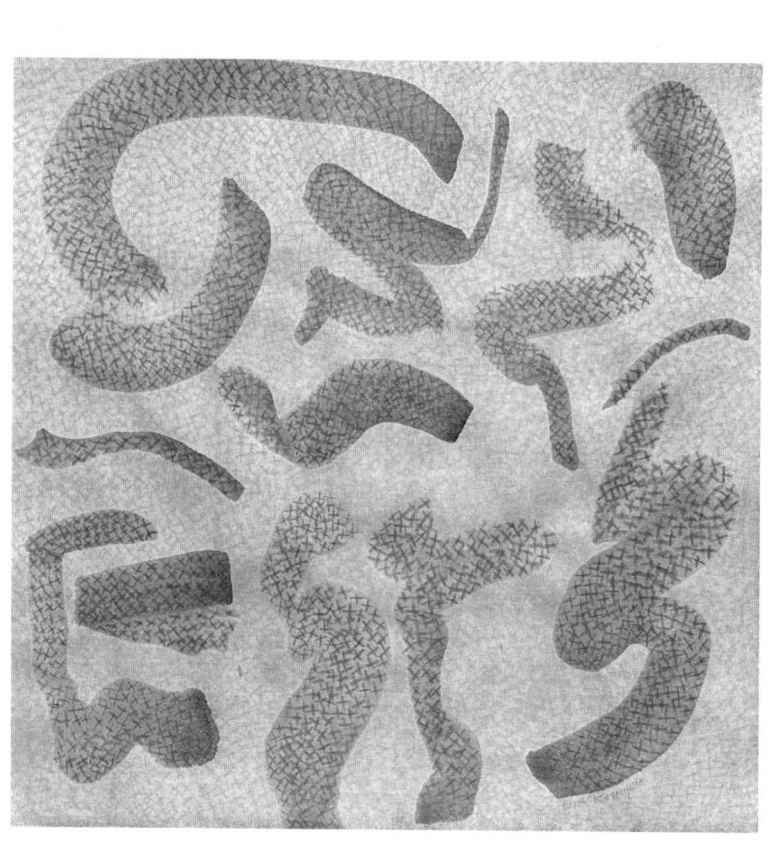

Splinters
&
Streams

Daphne Marlatt

chax 2025

Text copyright © 2025 by Daphne Marlatt
All rights reserved.

Cover and frontispiece images from paintings by Linda Rosenfield. Copyright © 2025 by the artist.

ISBN 978-1-946104-61-8
Poetry/Literature

Chax Press
6181 E 4th St
Tucson Arizona 85711-1613
USA

Chax Press is a nonprofit 501(c)3 arts organization. Chax Press books are supported in part by individual donors and by sales of the books. Please visit *https://chax.org/membership-support/* if you would like to contribute to our mission to make an impact on literature and culture in our time.

In the past two years Chax has received grant support from the Arizona Commission on the Arts, the Arts Foundation for Tucson and Southern Arizona, and The Poetry Foundation.

We thank our supporters, who make our work possible.

when the void of the page meets the splintering force of the line

Gaia Thomas

I digress

> *We are creatures of digression.*
> Jaspreet Singh

under soil cover
    roots web to surface blue
        peri's around

                winkling a way up

      tenders a petal tender
          untoward

                [splash of water on page
                [actual

                      accident, what is?

so i digress
      stray extend around

late mourning lines for
earth's wreckage

                    digging it up
oil drill seismic elephant footing

this web outreach
                toughing it up

under green blue sensate

                              yes & no
egress from this
                tangle

branchlets away from

                      simply to go   transgress
you snail-like

                vinca binding or some say creeping

myrtle hardy (mirthful
                            (hardly...

periwinkle blue fashion

I digress, I fictitious in face of
this

        to weed : to will

        some other design over
        blue upstart communal
        tracery

out of air [earth]
                     unseen roots and branches of sense

where Duncan's monarchs sailed
                     over *flowery markets* since

fallen

yet to inscribe, persist in
                 this mesh this broken
                             -ness

re-cess 'I'

    step back from
    intent to

        note / take

            birch leaf shimmy

    here as drought

        changes who or what's
        solid co-
            laps around

                anger as constant
                fossil pumps

        I inter-

    face stuck struck by
    percept glass as that

                        nameless wing drop

            transient here it's

flicker habit sip at
birch hole
        dry
    now summer rains ab sunt

            frogs

                      across that junction

this hand its take
on what
pencil thought erased

                    that quick

listen

    spring's leafing out

                        syntax leaps

    tenuous cross space green

                                  not the same

    calls variant

                      listener imbued

    4-year old's hysteric sidewalk squat

            tired or

    home terroir bound to boredom

        is that all

    this petal storm wind's not so
        gentle caress

                or crow cacophony
                   signals what

     say digress
            not the issue

out of mouths' too quick

                        to assess

what's meant

       to enter / intra-

laced say

temporal

hum body's resonance in different pitches assorted bodies seated practice
mist through windows leafless skeletal inside we turn *bhramari* nasal
lips oral rib cavities brummm a drum specific and local clears internal
brume vaguely out there once *brumaire* in France's calendar revolution
so temporal wheel this body settles in early October fog and still it's
student cafeteria smoke wet wool long hair in dread we wait the end
of Sixties Cuban missile crisis SDS now Study Direct Stream for Asian
students who walk the mist we walked and still catalpa trees drip global
warming lone autumn rose a faded bookmark yet no notion standing wet
this was /is Musqueam ground

what might be

fragile and too sparse for cloud effect *kanzakura* is it? almost white
stamen punctuated scattered blossom-float ahead some already shed
shredding weeks of petal light on dark pine shadow we walk on

more likely *prunus mume* delicate Friend of Winter skirting pine's
heavy branch so *meihau* resilient and persevering so Lin Bu's
"scattered shadows" luminous here its starburst stamens predict
more apricot than plum ah those

small wine-coloured ones we kids picked from garden prunus
wondering plums? knowing nothing of *umeboshi*'s pucker lips
or Lin Bu's moonlit view or winter's delicate apparition

these generations mashed in late spring rains

ghost presence on an East End street a fragile future these eyes
caress "the pathos of things" and their return through indifferent
fog rain onslaught frost a promise holding what might be in this
eleventh hour of earth bloom

park heart

so park your heart where green's celebrants race joyous four-legged
open mouth grin for frisbee leaps or luscious slow back rolls while
at ease their owners weather in neighborhood news stand posts for
circle chase joy barks

                        or later others park themselves by backstop
fence now ball unused once sheet-draped community film show grass
(old slang) seated viewers drawn from house surround

                                      or king voice
booming chair enthroned sunsoaker anecdotals to wheelchair bound
and younger female audients or greet boy neighbor come to show
hey great new bike eh?

                            crow chatter loud above unheard

the old chestnuts fall

sing chickadee sing

        for Kiku Hawkes'
        Gold Mountain Tableaux

once here all onces shot
in memoriam pictures how we
got to here required the new
did it? "free" (weigh) years of
"closing soon"

        a numbers toss gone home
        to cleared ground

        sing chickadee sing

for peanuts say debt once
repayable in the old demolish
and build extend or reno
heritage colours now

        crow logo promise
        the Crawl this hood's
        communal bird

or long for elsewhere *Paris* say
scrawled by the well-worn busted
urn (Creek Flats the cows would
graze that old) home to

                wing east crow to
                nightfall roost

closed-in porches opened up
choy sum plots long gone
now blue fescue garden scape
solar roof panel glow

                sing chickadee flit
                erratic gain

communitas in cappucino or what's
in common say inner city visitants now
slug beer down or wander alone aloud
crack'd

                sing chickadee sing
                for those still here

simply as

> *the breath-world / seeded / placed / piece after piece*
> Fred Wah

wind tree rustle rimming this park's joyous hubbub one-block green
pierced by kid cries a dad's indulgent laugh dog bark a skimming
Frisbee someone's mom pulls her child from hysterical play as
wind catches our blind in repeated knocking …

piece after piece

who planted those giant chestnut trees? who recalls the residents of
wooden houses firewood stacks small veggie plots long hours in
laundry shops?-- this whole block cleared to make what?

a park

time's signature

as change in today's rhythm arrives with warm weather alkies
waterpark play odd music outbursts morning tai chi midnight screams
'you fuckin asshole'…

resonant through body this block's inner-city
breathing day to day

how talk?

    they haven't heard a party line
    he didn't get she's cakin' it

          sun glow through smoke's

              vermillion

millions cached in Caribbean banks
Pakistani deaths in Sind monsoon

waste wood blaze beside this
river's smeared sprawl as

light-struck forest fires fire up

so dis this

disconnect

on dry

West Coast cedar rust ghosts
register shock in still green
rainforest abundant we thought
five to one hundred fifty year-old
small or tall these ones
gone dry-back gone headline

clouds don't rain

        nostalgie's musical repeat this
        child body's stored downpour rhythm round
        house eave drop frog sound chorale

symphonic yes

now-body's drawn to
rainforest biome's
unspoken rhyme

going going un-home

p.s.

hier's

        ayer
        aqua

vitae

        as if

in other words

               for Lorine Niedecker

almost downtown, certainly eastside in early morning's transparent light from the tip of a fir, above rooftop streetside murmur repeat mourning or calling, collared and intimate. coo and bill, coo. COOO the where-ARE-you dove.

in a stand of trees at the foot of a Wisconsin field with baby son in my arms, listen, listen, the owls are calling, the only bird of poetry Duncan said. for v-ow'l breath sings through open sounds or spirit holes in the small chitter of everyday field creature gossip.

so I said to Cid visiting with Shizumi, come hear the owls as we walked to that stand of trees. Cid never said or didn't know (so urban we were) those are wood doves calling, owls don't flock. we talked about Lorine who wasn't well, they were on their way to see her on Blackhawk Island, this poet who knew birds and water, flocks of, flecks of light.

so how had I forgotten the doves? Malaysia's spotted one, singing its name *terkukur* from the durian tree, one in a drench of song we would wake to liquid notes around the open verandah then…

but now is now, a raptor sound these collared doves also emit, ghost pterosaur staking its territory diminished scale, hissy fit, and predatory -- for our time.

minding the gap

    red orange feather flare
    signal flicker at suet's
    hunger jabs

            his on park grass
            palm under cheek & no
                coat to cover
                      earth-bound
                this body

                at what juncture

                      words un-join

rapid fire smatter
Covid   Heat Dome   Emergency Shelters
crises chronic now

                chthonic furies in new form

revenge imaginary rights to self to what
homeland laid waste

                earth surfaces

and the sunyata physics of pond plants

re mind

Indra netting 'I'

    for Bridget

torn between connection & alienation forgetful
how they interact the smaller the larger resonance
wavering out past shoals of
unexamined attitudes

                    slow inner breath
                      dissolve

Indra milking "cloud-cows" ancient ice jams
unlocked river flow invoked the one less 'I'
than cosmic spider web dew-bright embrace
multi-dimensional shine each one reflects
facets of any 'other'

you of stardust
me in a flicker's wing

further common-tary

for Phyllis Webb

pines one could say
soul pines – but who?

is that you, Phyllis, your

Mulberry tree with innocent eyes
Catalpa with your huge hands

who wood not look back at you
your signatory glance

enmeshed in our blue planet
now ransacked

your *interstellar longings*

for mutual recognition
each to each

without name and /or

more simply let's say
sheer event

much later

      for Roy Kiyooka

leaving soon? who knows when
my last train will bolt from this
birch-leaf locale

each hovering bee a green hurrah
now we

register mirage as *this*
this here
              still

despite
clime's downward slope

eye dance brims
eyes' transience

       (you on the far

side of this page your
pear tree gone

i'm reading background pines
new cones' sudden light

as cloud-lid shift macula registers
through glass this *this*
we think continuous

pandemic re-cognize

no inter
        face we go   squirrel bounce
        tree to tree unfelt even
        meme addict screen bound

                inside the long
        susurrus of nightfall

enter
        out where seawolf
        salmon bear coniferous
        domain inter are
        sans unique lordship ha!
        that old still perpetuate
        profit's suzeraineship

        yesterday's *hier* not higher
        arkes let's say

interim
        now enter en-terre'd
        skin's response to what's
        underfoot what grows what fruits
        and stirs in this

        within/without

sit

distant ting-ring crossing
flatcar rumble streets away
this traffic muffle sky-train screech

close up how Are ya? sidewalk hails
this four-square block i'm ghost to/
part of
        ears aloft years now
this sit this space above

is pan / all
        peopled in

mind's scramble

endemic this
populous a

permeable space

sources for quotes

Book epigraph from Gaia Thomas' essay "O Kylix" quoted in Sharon Thesen's October 29 2022 Olson Lecture at Cape Ann Museum Library and Archives, Gloucester, Mass.

"I digress"
epigraph from Jaspreet Singh's memoir, *My Mother, My Translator* (Vehicule Press: Montreal, 2021), p. 77. quoted lines from Robert Duncan, "Roots and Branches," title poem of *Roots and Branches* (New Directions, 1964) p. 3.

"what might be"Lin Bu (967-1028) wrote a classic poem about plum blossom,"Shan Yuan Xiao Mei," that has been translated many ways. "scattered shadows" is from Red Pine's translation (2013) quoted in Anne Lu's discussion of several translations of that poem, see https://thediagram.com/18_6/rev_lu.html

"sing chickadee sing"
an earlier version of this poem appeared in *Gold Mountain Tableaux*, a series of black and white photographs of Vancouver's East End Strathcona neighbourhood by Kiku Hawkes, self-published 2018.

"simply as"
epigraph taken from Fred Wah's *Earth*, 1974, unpaginated, reproduced in his *Scree, The Collected Earlier Poems, 1962-1991*, ed. Jeff Derksen (Vancouver: Talonbooks, 2015).

"minding the gap"
quote from Michael McClure's "Flower Garland Froth," *Mule Kick Blues and Last Poems* (City Lights Publishers: San Francisco, 2021) p. 63.

"further common-tary"
quoted lines from Phyllis Webb's *Water and Light: Ghazals and Anti Ghazals* (Coach House Press: Toronto, 1984), untitled poem, p. 45.

author acknowledgments

"I digress" was first published in the 50th Anniversary Issue 1/3 Spring 2022 of The Capilano Review.

None of these poems would have been written without the time my spouse Bridget MacKenzie cleared for me. Bridget died in June of 2022 so this collection is also in memory of her.

With gratitude to Charles Alexander and Chax Press for creating such a beautiful home for this work.

chax press

Founded in 1984 in Tucson, Arizona, Chax has published more than 250 books in a variety of formats, including hand printed letterpress books and chapbooks, hybrid chapbooks, book arts editions, and trade paperback editions such as the book you are holding. From August 2014 until July 2018 Chax Press resided in the University of Houston-Victoria Downtown Center for the Arts. Chax is a nonprofit 501c3 organization which depends on suppport from various government & private funders, and, primarly, from individual donors and readers. In July 2018 Chax Press returned to Tucson. In 2021, Chax Press founder and director Charles Alexander was awarded the Lord Nose Award for lifetime achievement in literary publishing.

Chax Press stands against all attacks on democracy, civil rights, and the dignity and self-determination of all peoples, in the USA and internationally. We stand against authoritarian government, including that which exists within supposedly democratic systems. We stand against all genocides, including the one being enacted presently in Gaza against the Palestinian people. We stand for equal human rights for all, and we encourage and believe in peace and love as critical to solving problems in our world.

Splinters & Streams was originally forecast as a Chax letterpress book, but with intervening studio moves and set-ups, we have decided to release it as the book you are now holding.

Splinters & Streams has been designed by Charles Alexander. The cover drawing by Linda Rosenfield was generously donated by the artist. Type for text of the poems is Albertina Pro, with Gill Sans Light used for titling. The book is printed by KC Book Manufacturing in Summer 2025.

Thanks go to all of those who support Chax Press, and to Daphne Marlatt for the chance to work with her poetry.

Our current mailing address is 6181 East 4th Street, Tucson, Arizona 85711-1613. You can email us at *chaxpress@chax.org*. Find CHAX online at *https://chax.org*

150 copies released in the initial edition/printing.

The current copy is 110 of 150.